In Pursuit of His Presence

Foreword

Greetings in the name of our Lord and savior Jesus Christ. Grace, mercy, and peace be unto you my father's children. There, is a profound premise that all things that embodies our human existence is based on striving toward excellence. Excellence in God's word and in his ways can be achieved by aligning our mind, body, and soul with the matchless word of God.

This is a culmination of acknowledgement, reverence, and confession with the pursuit of love, joy, peace, and happiness that are some of the foundations that help in reaching for the greater height in God. I believe embracing these attributes will begin the alignment of being in God's presence. These devotional, inspirational, and empowering passages you are about to embark upon in this book is a collection of teaching which will assist you in the pursuit to be in God's presence.

The authors are all ordained elders in the Southern Assembly Church of Christ, Disciples of Christ Eastern District of America, Inc. They are intercessors for the church, prayer partners, and prayer warriors for those who need someone to touch and agree. These elders are faith-based believers of whom are strong supporters of the ministries. These, authors are educated and well renowned leaders in our church and the community. They also have a very strong GODLY presence in their homes and with their families. This book will be an asset in your pursuit to being in God's presence. I believe these authors will edify the world in which we live in today!

Bishop Ronnie L Hood, Presiding Prelate

In Pursuit of His Presence

Trudy Askew Robinson
Constance Hamilton McCloud
Tonya Parker Davis

In Pursuit of His Presence

https://www.facebook.com/2021inpursuitofhispresence/

Copyright © 2021 Trudy Askew Robinson, Constance Hamilton McCloud, Tonya Parker Davis

All rights reserved.

ISBN: 978-0-578-84402-2

Unless otherwise noted, Scripture references are from The Holy Bible, New International Version, NIV. Copyright 1973, 1978, 1984 by Biblica, Inc. Used by permission of Zondervan. All rights reserved worldwide. Other Scriptures are taken from The Holy Bible, King James Version (KJV). The New King James Version (NKJV). Copyright 1982 by Thomas Nelson, Inc. Used by permission.

Table of Contents

PURSUIT (MEANING) 6
THINGS TO REMEMBER 7
PURSUIT CHALLENGE 8
DAY 1 9
DAY 2 11
DAY 3 13
DAY 4 15
DAY 5 17
DAY 6 19
DAY 7 21
DAY 8 23
DAY 9 25
DAY 10 27
DAY 11 29
DAY 12 32
DAY 13 34
DAY 14 36
DAY 15 38
DAY 16 40
DAY 17 42
DAY 18 44
DAY 19 46
DAY 20 48
DAY 21 51
DAY 22 53

In Pursuit of His Presence

DAY 23	55
DAY 24	57
DAY 25	59
DAY 26	61
DAY 27	63
DAY 28	65
DAY 29	67
DAY 30	69
DAY 31	71
ACKNOWLEDGEMENTS	73
ABOUT THE AUTHORS	74

Let's consider the word Pursuit

Pursuit is the action of following after someone or something, with the intent of capturing it. Especially in a chase it may be a goal, dream, or an idea. This devotional is focused on God and knowing his path in our daily lives, as we walk it out.

Track your steps

Use the space at the end of each devotional to document your journey and record your thoughts. Track your steps on your Pursuit of His Presence.

Things to remember as you embark on this pursuit

- God's word is powerful. It is alive and gives us fresh revelation. Have great expectations.

- We start each day of this devotional with a scripture to help you with the daily chase.

- We end each daily devotional with prayer. Prayer changes things.

- Your Pursuit of God is a lifelong journey. It is our pleasure to support your journey with this 31-day devotional. We encourage you to continue what you have started.

In Pursuit of His Presence

Pursuit Challenge Accepted

I, _____, accept this challenge.
          YOUR NAME

I know this pursuit will take time and dedication, but I will continue to strive and get in pursuit to be able to be blessed in his presence.

_____
Signature

_____
Date

In Pursuit of His Presence

DAY 1

THE POWER OF HIS PRESENCE

One thing I ask of the Lord, this is what I seek, that I may dwell in the house of the Lord all the days of my life, to gaze upon the beauty of the Lord and to seek him in his temple.

Psalm 27:4

Have the pressures of life ever weighed you down to the point that you needed to feel the presence of the Lord? With all the responsibilities in life, I often find myself hastening to the throne of God. His presence is my safe haven. It's the place I run to when I need to experience his power. In my safe haven, I find peace, and happiness. The Lord has a sweet way of calming all my fears and removing my doubts. Just knowing that He is present reassures me that He loves me, and He cares. I count it a privilege to abide in the presence of the Lord, and I invite you to experience the power of being in his presence.

My Prayer with You

Heavenly Father, we thank you for allowing your children access to your presence. In your presence we receive the fullness of joy, and at your right hand are pleasures forever more. We are grateful that we can come boldly to your throne of grace, to obtain mercy and grace to help us in a time of need. We endeavor to seek your face early in the morning, and throughout the day. We thank you for opportunity to experience the power of your presence. This is our prayer ... in Jesus Name, Amen.

Reading: Psalm 27:4-5, Psalm 16:11, and Hebrew 4:16

TRACK YOUR STEPS:

In Pursuit of His Presence

DAY 2

PURSUE THE PERSPECTIVE OF GOD

But seek first his Kingdom and his righteousness, and all these things will be given to you as well.

Matthew 6:33

Every day we are confronted with challenges, opposition, as well as opportunities. Life in general can be overwhelming! In all of these things, we must first pursue the perspective of God. It is important that we understand what our Heavenly Father has to say about the affairs that govern our lives. Instead of asking our friends or colleagues, ask God!

How much better would life be if we pursue the perspective of our Heavenly Father. When we seek his face, he steps right in and directs our paths. Yes, it is human nature to worry, but why should we spend time worrying; when we serve a God who will work all things for our good?

My Prayer with You

Abba Father, we are indeed grateful to you for supplying all of our needs. Today we repent of time spent worrying. Please forgive us for failure of acknowledging you in all of our ways. Today, we cast all of our cares and concerns at the foot of the cross and we leave them there. Today, we seek your perspective in our lives. We ask you in faith to give us this day our daily bread. We thank you, for being the Good Shepherd who cares deeply for your sheep. We give your name praise, honor, and glory in Jesus Name, Amen.

Reading: Matthew 6:33, Proverbs 3:5-6, 1 Peter 5:7, John 10:11

TRACK YOUR STEPS:

DAY 3

THE ANTIDOTE FOR ANXIETY

Do not be anxious about anything, but in every situation, by prayer and petition, with thanksgiving, present your requests to God. And the peace of God, which transcends all understanding, will guard your hearts and your minds in Christ Jesus.

Philippians 4:6-7

Prayer has become my antidote to anxiety. An antidote is something that is used to counteract a problem. Often times when we incur problems, we become anxious. Let me encourage you to give your problems to God through prayer. This allows you to relinquish control and to give God full authority to handle our affairs. As we allow the Lord to exercise his power, our propensity to worry lessens. As we follow the scriptural algorithm, the outcome will result in peace. Therefore, we don't need to worry, all we need to do is pray!

My Prayer with You

Heavenly Father, we are fortunate to call you Savior, and Lord. We thank you for being mindful of us. Your word declares that we should always pray and not give up. We thank you for the provision of prayer. We are forever indebted to you for not only hearing our prayers but answering them. Today, we cast all of our cares upon you, for your word declares that you care for us. We give you complete control to reign and rule over the affairs of our lives. We thank you for providing the antidote for anxiety, and we receive the peace that far exceeds our understanding. We decree and declare that we will not panic, but we will pray, in Jesus Name. Amen.

Reading: Philippians 4:6-7, Luke 18:1, Psalm 8:4

TRACK YOUR STEPS:

DAY 4

INVITE THE INTERCESSOR IN

In the same way, the Spirit helps us in our weakness. We do not know what ought to pray for, but the Spirit himself intercedes for us through wordless groans. And he who searches our heart knows the mind of the Spirit, because the Spirit intercedes for God's people in accordance with the will of God.

Romans 8:26-28

As the years continues to unfold, I am appreciative for the Holy Spirit's presence in my life. Often times the pressures of this world, can leave me without mere words. It is during these times that I extend an invitation to the Holy Spirit to intercede or speak to God on my behalf. There are also those times when I do not even realize what I need. But I am grateful that when I don't know, the Holy Spirit always knows, and it is at work behind the scenes. He knows our current, past, and future petitions, and he will intervene on our behalf.

As Christians we must come to identify and invite the Holy Spirit to intercede for us. Today, I beseech you to receive the Spirit of Christ, and welcome him to petition the Lord on your behalf. The bible tells us that the Holy Spirit will lead us into all truth. Once we receive the truth, we must abide in it. The Lord has given us access to his Spirit and power. I encourage you to welcome the Spirit of Christ to intercede for you! Will you invite the intercessor in?

My Prayer with You

Heavenly Father, we are grateful to you, for the gift of the Holy Spirit, who makes intercessions for us. We thank you for our mediator who knows what we need when we needed it. Spirit of the Living God, we thank you for speaking for us when we do not have the ability, to speak. We are grateful to you for advocating on our behalf, when have no idea what we need. We invite you to have thine own way in our lives. This we pray in the powerful name of Jesus Amen.

Reading: Romans 8:26-28, John 16:13

TRACK YOUR STEPS:

DAY 5

FOLLOW THE SHEPHERD'S LEAD

He restoreth my soul; he leadeth me in the paths of righteousness for his name's sake.

Psalm 23:3

I have come to appreciate the role and relationship that a Shepherd has with his sheep. A Shepherd is a nurturer, nourisher, protector, and provider. Just as the Lord restored David, he will also provide rest for our souls. When we get exhausted or become weary; have confidence that the Good Shepherd will provide a place of renewal and restoration. The Lord is our Shepherd, and he will lead us in the pathway of righteousness. We can only live a righteous life with the help of a righteous God. Following his lead means carrying out the instructions that you receive through prayer, mediation, and studying the word of God. Our Heavenly Father, desires to lead, and guide us to be righteous in his sight. So, before we take an alternate path, follow the Shepherd's lead!

My Prayer with You

Sovereign Lord, we thank you for loving us and leading us into the path of righteousness, for your name sake. We admit that we can do nothing without you, but with you, we can do all things! Today, we affirm that you are our Shepherd. Help us to hear your voice and not a voice of a stranger. Continue to nourish and lead us into green pastures. When we become weary, lead us beside the still waters and restore our souls. Help us to follow your lead! We thank you for caring so greatly for us, and for providing everything that we need. In Jesus name we pray, Amen.

Reading: Psalm 23:1-6

TRACK YOUR STEPS:

In Pursuit of His Presence

DAY 6

AN OPEN INVITATION

Come to me, all you who are weary and burdened, and I will give you rest. Take my yoke upon you and learn from me, for I am gentle and humble in heart and you will find rest for your souls. For my yoke is easy and my burden is light.

Matthew 11:28-30

Are you tired and heavy ladened with the cares of this world? If so, Jesus extends an open invitation to you! Yes, you… you can come to him. One day, I found myself in that place. I was sick and tired of navigating the pitfalls of life, and I needed a drastic change. I fell on my knees and I cried out to the Lord. I came to him as a sinner in need of his saving grace. That day, Jesus welcomed me with open arms as a Father waiting patiently to receive his child. In Him I found rest for my weary soul.

If you find yourself in that place today, I invite you to come to Jesus. He extends to you and open invitation and he bids you to come.

My Prayer with You

Heavenly Father, I thank you for extending an open invitation to your children to come to you when we are burdened with the troubles of this world. It is comforting to know that you love us, and you care. This life is hectic, and we need your help!

In Pursuit of His Presence

Today, we put on the yoke of salvation, and we receive rest for our souls. We offer this prayer in Jesus' name, Amen.

Reading: Matthew 11:28-30

TRACK YOUR STEPS:

In Pursuit of His Presence

DAY 7

SEASONS CHANGE

For everything there is a season and a time for every purpose under heaven.

Ecclesiastes 3:1

The earth transitions through four seasons each year. Each season is unique as it presents changes and challenges of nature, related to the climate. The winter tends to be the coldest of all seasons, and summer is the warmest. In the spring flowers and plants bloom. During the fall, the leaves turn colors, the final crops are harvested, and leaves fall from the trees.

Thus, is the life of a Christian. There will be various seasons of our lives. One day we can literally be on top of the world, and the next day in the valley. One day we can be in optimal health and then the next, our health may fail. The good news is seasons change. No matter what we go through, remain optimistic and take the high road. We must come to understand that it's just a season, and seasons change!

My Prayer with You

Heavenly Father, we thank you for being our Rock of Ages. We rejoice and find comfort in knowing that you are with us through the many seasons of our lives. We are forever indebted to you for carrying us through each transition of life. We trust in you, for you are our Savior, Deliverer, and Lord. We thank you for being God in the mountain and God in the valley. We are grateful that you cause the seasons of life to change. And it is reassuring to know that trouble and trials do not last always. Thank you for causing us to triumph over our trials, and giving us victory through your Son, Jesus Christ. Amen.

Reading: Ecclesiastes 3:1-8

TRACK YOUR STEPS:

DAY 8

PRAYER AND PRAISE AT MIDNIGHT

And at midnight Paul and Silas prayed, and sang praises unto God: and the prisoners heard them. And suddenly there was a great earthquake, so that the foundations of the prison were shaken: and immediately all the doors were opened, and every one's bands were loosed.

Acts 16:25-26

At some point in our lives, all of us will experience the "midnight hour." Midnight is time of transition between night and day. Thomas Fuller, a great historian once said, "the darkest hour is just before the dawn." With that thought in mind, we can petition God through prayer asking him to bring us through the dark times of life. And finally, we can praise him for the light that is sure to come.

My Prayer with You

Today's Prayer: Heavenly Father, I thank you for my midnight experiences. It is during these times that I've learned to seek your face even the more. It is during these times, that I have become desperate for you. Thank you for unlocking the chains of bondage and setting me free. I give you glory for answering my prayers and elevating my praise, In Jesus Name… Amen.

In Pursuit of His Presence

Reading: Acts 16:25-26

TRACK YOUR STEPS:

DAY 9

USE YOUR WEAPON

Put on the whole armour of God, that ye may be able to stand against the wiles of the devil.

Ephesians 6:11

All of us, at some point in our lives, have come under a spiritual attack of the adversary. What weapons did you utilize to combat the enemy?

As Christians we are discouraged from utilizing physical force to fight our battles; therefore, we must utilize our spiritual weapons if we desire to win spiritual battles. Ephesians 6:10 encourages us to put on the whole armor of God that we might be able to stand against the wiles or the tricks of the enemy. What good is a soldier's weapon if he/she doesn't use it? If you are feeling defeated, let me encourage you to use your weaponry.

My Prayer with You

Omniscient and Omnipotent God, I thank you for ruling and reigning in my life. Thank you for providing the weapons of warfare. Help me to armor up every day and to use my spiritual weapons to defeat the enemy. I give you glory, honor, and praise. In Jesus Name. Amen.

In Pursuit of His Presence

Reading: Ephesians 6:10-18

TRACK YOUR STEPS:

In Pursuit of His Presence

DAY 10

FORSAKING ALL TO FOLLOW CHRIST

As Jesus started on his way, a man ran up to him and fell on his knees before him. "Good teacher, "he asked, "what must I do to inherit eternal life?

Mark 10:17

We must realize that our day of reckoning is soon to come. Have you ever asked the question, "What must I do to inherit eternal life?" As we read the Bible, it is evident that we must forsake all, to follow Christ. To gain eternal life, we must surrender our lives, in every aspect. Jesus declared in Matthew 16:25, for whoever wants to save their life will lose it, but whoever loses their life for me will find it.

Are you willing to forsake all and follow Christ? Jesus gave us the ultimate example as he gave his life for the sins of the world. In doing so, he opened the door of eternal life for all. The bible declares in Romans 10: 9-10, that if we confess with our mouth that Jesus is Lord, and believe in our heart, that God raised him from the dead, you will be saved. For it is with your heart that you believe, and are justified, and it is with your mouth that you profess your faith and are saved.

In Pursuit of His Presence

My Prayer with You

Eternal God our Father, we thank you for giving your only begotten Son, Jesus Christ, that whosoever believeth in him would have eternal life. We confess that Jesus suffered, bled, and died on the cross for the sins of mankind. Without the shedding of his blood there would be no remission of our sins. Jesus, we thank you for forsaking all, so that we might have eternal life. We ask that you forgive us of our sins and give us the power to die to our will, to forsake all, in order that we might follow you. We invite the Spirit of Christ to abide in us, to lead and guide us and govern our character, so that it aligns with our confession. We thank you and we humbly pray this prayer in your Son, Jesus' Name. Amen.

Reading: Mark 10:17-31, Matthew 16:25, John 3:16, Romans 10:9-10

TRACK YOUR STEPS:

DAY 11

IF HE BRINGS YOU TO IT, HE WILL BRING YOU THROUGH IT

Then Joshua rose early in the morning; and they set out from Acacia Grove and came to the Jordan, he and all the children of Israel, and lodged there before they crossed over. So it was, after three days, that the officers went through the camp; and they commanded the people, saying, "When you see the ark of the covenant of the Lord your God, and the priests the Levites, bearing it, then you shall be a space between you and it, about two thousand cubits by measure. Do not come near it, that you may know the way by which you must go, for you have not passed this way before.

Joshua 3:1-4

Have you ever found yourself facing an impossible impassable situation? A time when you were so overwhelmed by life that you were not sure what to do? I've been there and done that. I couldn't go back, because there was nothing to go back to. I couldn't move forward, because I didn't know how. I felt stuck. All I knew to do was admire the chaos that was before me.

Joshua the newly appointed leader and the entire nation had a similar experience. They were confronted with the Jordan River. The Jordan seemingly stood between the nation of Israel and the promised land. There they were, facing a massive obstacle. It was flood season for the Jordan. Its swift flowing waters were full of debris with currents that reached up to 40-miles an hour. The plain that surrounds this river was packed with tangled brush and dense growth. The Jordan had swelled its banks, spreading about a mile across, ranging in depth from 3ft to 12ft. It lay right in front of them. It was a dangerous intimidating sight.

They camped there for three days admiring the problem. Watching it overflow its banks. The river must have seemed impossible to overcome. They must have thought, how are we going to get through this? How often have you had that same question about the obstacles you've faced? The ultimate question for them was could they trust God with their impossible situation? Can you trust God despite what you see? Will you trust God to be faithful in the face of great difficulty? Just as God led the children of Israel through the Jordan River, He faithfully leads us through the difficulties we face. My experience with God tells me that If He brings you to it, He will bring you through it.

My Prayer with You

Faithful Father, I acknowledge your good plan for my life. Lord help me this day and every day to trust you to overcome every obstacle in my life. Amen.

Reading: Joshua 3:1-13, Joshua 4:23-24

TRACK YOUR STEPS:

DAY 12

WILL YOU BE MADE WHOLE?

When Jesus saw him lie, and knew that he had been now a long time in that case, he saith unto him, Wilt thou be made whole?

John 5:6

In Jerusalem there was a place set aside for those that suffered with chronic illness and debilitation. A pool was their gathering spot. When Jesus arrived, he found a man and asked him the simplest question: "Will you be made whole?" It was a direct question. Would you like to receive what you've been waiting for? The man didn't answer yes. Instead, he gave a reason why he continued in the current condition. "There is no help for me!"

The name of the pool was Bethesda. Bethesda means house of grace or house of mercy. The name of the pool gives a hint of the encounter that was about to take place. Whenever Jesus arrives, mercy and grace are sure to arrive as well. The place was described to have five porches. In scripture the number five is representative of Grace. Grace always brings blessings. This man didn't go looking for Jesus, Jesus came to Him. He didn't even know who Jesus was. How much more will Jesus extend grace of deliverance to those that belong to him?

After his encounter with Jesus, immediately the man was made whole. That problem he woke up with that morning, the one he carried around with him for 38 years was gone. Friend, can we talk? There is deliverance available to the people of God, so why are you in that same space and spot? Without excuse, go ahead and say yes to God. Receive the grace for healing and wholeness. God is your present help. Rise up-Move forward in God.

My Prayer with You

Lord help me to change my thinking that I may have great expectation of the great things you can do in my life. Amen.

Reading John 5:1-15

TRACK YOUR STEPS:

In Pursuit of His Presence

DAY 13

A PROMISE IS A PROMISE

For all the promises of God in him are yea, and in him Amen, unto the glory of God by us.

2 Corinthians 1:20

Kelcee, my granddaughter is 5 years old. She asks, "Can you come and pick me up?" Or she asks, "Gigi can you buy this for me?" I say "yes." And to that answer she will say, "You promise?" She wants assurance. Like Kelcee, we also like assurances. We can be sure that a promise is a promise when it is from God.

A promise includes a declaration and a deed. When you make a promise, you say what you are going to do and then you do what you say. Paul declared that God is faithful to His promises. All the promises of God in Jesus are yea and amen.

The word translated to *yea* means *sure*, and the word translated to *amen* means *firm*. This scripture assures us that all God's promises and His word are sure and firm. They are unchanging, unwavering, and unmovable. Whether a blessing or in judgement, His word will not return void. For the sake of His Name, He will fulfill His promises.

God wants us to be without doubt concerning His promises. Therefore, to convince us of the faithfulness of His promises, God gave us His oath. God's promises are a declaration by Him. His promises cover His plans for us. They tell us what we can expect from Him. God said it, so surely, He will do it. God has declared some things over our lives. You want to know more about those promises? The Bible is the book of promises.

My Prayer with You

Dear Lord, your word is immutable, your character unchangeable, and your precious promises are sure. Lord help me to stand on your promises and embrace your plans for my life. Amen.

Reading: 2 Corinthians 1:18-22
Jeremiah 31:31–33 Hebrews 6:13-20

TRACK YOUR STEPS:

In Pursuit of His Presence

DAY 14

THE LORD OUR STRENGTH

There is none holy as the Lord: for there is none beside thee: neither is there any rock like our God.

1 Samuel 2:2

How great is our God! His greatness, His awesome power is beyond our ability to adequately describe. He gives us strength even at our most desperate points. He is our rock and fortress. When we need refuge, we go to Him in prayer. Hannah was a praying woman. Out of the abundance of her sorrow she poured out her soul to God. She petitioned God who was the only one that could solve her problem. There are some things that only God can do. The sooner we embrace that truth the sooner we will find rest in Him. Hannah left her worship experience encouraged, comforted with the blessing of the Lord. God heard her petition and answered her prayer.

Hannah conceived and gave birth to Samuel. She nurtured her son Samuel for three years and left him at the temple of God, fulfilling her vow. Hannah gave back to God that which she most wanted but she didn't leave feeling emptied or deprived. Instead, Hannah had a song of praise. Again, out of the abundance of her heart she worshipped God. In her prayer of Thanksgiving, she acknowledged that God is Holy (nobody is like our God). He is sovereign and delivers strength and rest to those that trust in Him.

In Pursuit of His Presence

In my life there have been many moments of desperate prayer. Though I didn't always get the answer I desired, I have always been strengthened by prayer.

My Prayer with You

Dear Lord in times when I find myself in anguish of soul, may I rush to you realizing that you are my source of comfort and strength. Amen.

Reading: Matthew 21:22, 1 Sam. 2:1-4, Psalm 61

TRACK YOUR STEPS:

DAY 15

GOD TAKES GREAT CARE OF US

What is man, that thou art mindful of him? And the son of man, that thou visitest him? For thou hast made him a little lower than the angels, and hast crowned him with glory and honor.

Psalm 8:4-5

David asked God the question, "What is man, that you are mindful of him? And the son of man, that you care for him?" In this psalm, David is filled with wonderment and admiration. He gazed at the night sky and began to consider the ways of God.

David had plenty of experience sleeping under an open sky. As a youth he tended his father's sheep under the heavens with only God to comfort him. It is there that he grew a heart of a warrior. David also lay before an open sky as he ran from King Saul. He was destined to be king, but he was living the life of a fugitive. David lost his way for a while during that season but even during his time as a bandit he learned to fully trust God. He learned how to encourage himself as he meditated on the faithfulness of God. And again, in Psalm 63 as an aging king, David was sleeping under the stars after fleeing from his own son. On this occasion we clearly see David's heart for worship. He found rest in God because he knew that only God could deliver the help he needed.

It is not known with certainty at what stage of David's life Psalm 8 was written but clearly David was in awe of God. As

In Pursuit of His Presence

David considered the majesty of the stars, moon, and all the marvelous works of God, he felt insignificant. David acknowledged the great care God has for his creation. God has lovingly crowned us with glory and honor. You and I have been crowned. That crown of glory and honor is God's investments in humans. The greatest honor of all is that while we were still sinners, Christ died for the likes of you and me. His son Jesus sacrificed it all to care for our greatest need, reconciliation to God our father.

My Prayer with You

Lord help me to realize my smallness in comparison to your greatness. I worship you because even though I am frail and flawed your thoughts toward me are precious and great is the sum of those thoughts. Father thank you because you have graciously cared for me, providing all my needs. Amen.

Reading: Psalm 8, Psalm 63, Psalm 139

TRACK YOUR STEPS:

In Pursuit of His Presence

DAY 16

TRUSTING GOD

What time I am afraid, I will trust in thee.

Psalm 56:3

King David has a heroic resume. He killed two of the most dangerous animals in the world. He was a giant slayer and a mighty warrior. There was a time when he was afraid. David was in a desperate situation and he made a desperate decision that he later regretted.

Saul threw a spear at David three times and he finally got the message. Realizing Saul wanted him dead, David made his escape. He thought that he could find refuge with the enemies of Israel. David went looking for a safe place to hide, but that backfired on him. Never ever run to the enemy. Always seek God. God alone is our refuge. He alone is our hiding place.

David was in real trouble. He was at the mercy of the Philistines and realized they were planning to kill him. David came to himself. He remembered who he was -the beloved one- the apple of God's eye. He put his trust where it should have been, in God almighty. David called on God. He understood that crying out to God made His enemies turn back. His trust in God gave him confidence. David went from being afraid to a confident declaration, "This I know, God is for me." Do you know God is for you? In those moments when fear tries to grip our hearts; we must remember that God is on our side.

My Prayer with You

Lord my God, be merciful to me. Thank you for being my present help in my time of trouble. Whatever times that I find myself afraid, I will trust in You. Amen.

Reading: Psalm 56, 1 Samuel 21:10-15, Psalm 34

TRACK YOUR STEPS:

DAY 17

CLINGING TO GOD

And Jacob was left alone; and there wrestled a man with him until the breaking of day. And when he saw that he prevailed not against him, he touched the hollow of his thigh; and the hollow of Jacob's thigh was out of joint, as he wrestled with him.

Genesis 32:24-25

The name Jacob means Heel Grabber a person that uses their strength to grasp hold of someone or something and hang on. Jacob lived up to his name. He was a wrestler. He wrestled with his brother in the womb. He wrestled with his father-in-law for his wives, and finally he wrestled with God. The event in the life of Jacob is a picture of God, our loving father striving with us in our imperfections. Despite our shortcomings and faults, God doesn't change His mind about us, instead God gives us grace.

At the breaking of day just as the sun was about to shine, and just before Jacob was able to see God's face; God let Jacob know it's time to end his wrestling career. He was saying enough is enough. It's time to end your struggle with me. Even though Jacob had loss. He prevailed. He kept hanging on. Jacob was clinging to God with all his strength. Jacob had been conquered by God. He had been apprehended. Jacob's clinging was acknowledging that he desperately needed God.

Jacob came to a place of submission. His demand for a blessing was not really a demand but a plea. He pleaded with God through his tears. Jacob cried out "I will not let You go unless You bless me." And God did bless Jacob. He changed him, and He signified it by changing Jacob's name. He said to him, "What is your name?" Jacob answered "Jacob." Jacob was forced to admit his sins and shortcomings.

We must confess before the Lord and allow God to change us. I have been there - It's me, it's me, it's me, oh Lord standing in the need of a blessing. We prevail with God when we first submit to Him and then hold on to our relationship with Him with all our might.

My Prayer with You

Lord, I can do nothing without you. My desire is to be transformed into who you created me to be. May your will for my life be done. Lord help me submit and hold on to you, never letting go. Amen.

Reading: Genesis 32:24-32, Hosea 12:3-4

TRACK YOUR STEPS:

DAY 18

OPENNESS TO GOD

And looking up to heaven, he sighed, and saith unto him, Ephphatha, that is, Be opened.

Mark 7:34

Ephphatha - the word uttered by Jesus to a deaf man. Ephphatha is the Greek form of an Aramaic word, meaning *Be opened*. It also means to be connected with another. Jesus' entire ministry is designed to connect us to His father.

The healings of Jesus Christ were recorded to serve a specific purpose. The miracles Jesus performed displayed His authority as the Son of God. Each healing came with a message, addressed a human condition, and confirmed who Jesus was.

The method that Jesus uses for healing this man was unique. The details of this interaction reveal to us that Jesus does not consider our cause as just another case but that He sees our unique makeup. He knows every believer for who we are and knows our special needs. This healing reminds us of the intimacy of our relationship with God and His son. Our healing, our place of brokenness is intensely personal. Jesus knows the intimate details of our issues. He has seen every slight, rejection, abuse, mistreatment and injury. He also knows our hopes and dreams.

Jesus leaned in close to the man and said Ephphatha. The message He conveys through this interaction is this; in order to get what we need most; we must open our hearts to receive Him. This willing connection becomes our life-giving source. We have to be opened to receive Jesus and all that He offers.

My Prayer with You

Lord, help me to search my heart. I yield all things that hinder my healing and wholeness. Thank you for touching my specific need and opening my heart so I can connect to you. I declare that you do all things well. Amen.

Reading: Mark 7: 31-37; John 1:1-12

TRACK YOUR STEPS:

DAY 19

WE ARE BETTER THAN BLESSED

Blessed be the God and Father of our Lord Jesus Christ, who hath blessed us with all spiritual blessings in heavenly places in Christ

Ephesians 1:3

Ephesians is the book to read if we ever have an identity crisis as children of God. It clearly tells us of who we are and the benefits of relationship with God our Father and Jesus our redeemer. Paul's epistle to the Ephesians provides instruction for walking worthy of our calling as followers of Jesus. We are encouraged to be both strong and steadfast. We are blessed by our father with all spiritual blessings in heavenly places in Christ: He has given us everything we need to walk this journey.

God chose us from the foundation of time to be Holy- set apart and blameless in His sight. Because of His love for us he predestined us to be a part of His family. It is so uplifting to know that it was God's good pleasure to blessed us with heavenly blessings. Our blessings are a purposeful act of God's will. It pleased him to do what He did for us.

If you have ever felt rejected or unwanted, know that God has always had you picked out to be His own. God has poured His love on us. It is unwavering, from everlasting to everlasting. In Him we have redemption through His blood and the forgiveness of sins, in accordance with the riches of God's grace. God is not stingy with His Grace, but he lavishes it on us. His grace is abundant and extensive.

How do you know if these riches in glory really belong to you? All you have to do is believe in the truth of the Gospel. If you believe it, live it. Do you believe? If yes, then these benefits of grace belong to you.

My Prayer with You

Father, I thank you for your gracious love toward me. Thank you for your keeping power and for the many blessings that are mine, because you chose me to be part of your family. Thank you that I am sealed until the day of redemption with the Holy ghost. Thank you that I am better than blessed. Amen.

Reading: Ephesians 1, Psalm 103

TRACK YOUR STEPS:

In Pursuit of His Presence

DAY 20

DRAW NEAR TO GOD

And Moses went up into the mount, and a cloud covered the mount. And the glory of the Lord abode upon mount Sinai, and the cloud covered it six days: and the seventh day he called unto Moses out of the midst of the cloud. And the sight of the glory of the Lord was like devouring fire on the top of the mount in the eyes of the children of Israel. And Moses went into the midst of the cloud, and gat him up into the mount: and Moses was in the mount forty days and forty nights.

Exodus 24: 15-18

Moses served as a mediator between God and his chosen people. God called Moses up to the mountain to talk with him, and then sent Moses back to relay his instructions to the people. The scene here in Exodus 24 takes place as Moses is sealing the covenant with the sacrificial blood. He sprinkles the blood on the people and later that day the elders enjoyed a meal in the presence of the Lord. This was a glorious experience for a select few. Those privileged to attend described seeing a pavement of sapphire, and it appeared as the clearest of blue skies. It was a glorious fellowship meal.

God separated Moses out for an even more intimate fellowship after that. He called Moses to come on up a little higher. The mountain was on fire, which produced a thick cloud of smoke. Moses was not able to see because of the smoke, but he went up there anyway. Up there surrounded by the glory of the Lord,

Moses and Joshua waited. For six days nothing happened. Oh, but on the 7th day God called out of the midst. What if Moses had not waited. He would have missed the call, the communion, the honor of being with God.

Drawing close to God produces a greater level of fellowship with God. It also introduces a greater level of sacrifice. Moses was gone 40 days and 40 nights without food or drink surviving on the glory of God. Moses had to give up some things, but it was worth it. Many times, God ask us to do things that are unfamiliar and uncomfortable. It requires faith and obedience.

Moses did what was required. He was purposeful in his efforts to draw near. God didn't come and get Moses; Moses had to rise up. God calls for us to draw near to Him. He is calling to us, "come up."

My Prayer with You

Lord, I delight in you. Help me to respond with obedience to your call for greater intimate fellowship. Amen.

Reading: Exodus 24

TRACK YOUR STEPS:

DAY 21

MINDSET AND ATTITUDE

Be strong and of good courage, fear not, nor be afraid of them: for the Lord thy God, he it is that doth go with thee; he will not fail thee, nor forsake thee

Deuteronomy 31:6

Mindset is your collection of thoughts and beliefs that shape the way you think. Attitude is your personal view and feelings of a situation, person, place or thing.

The COVID-19 virus, Quarantine of 2020, had taken a toll on the whole world, the nation and even me. I was not immune to the stress of it. It had eroded some of my "Godfidence", as I sat at my newly assigned post taking non-touch temperatures. Up walks, the chaplain with a conversation about the same bible verses and personality that I was studying, and that was Joshua.

The chaplain confirmed that God told Joshua at least five times, "Not to Fear!" My mindset and attitude about my situation had to change. I had to believe what God had said in his word during troubling times. I began to say to myself, "No fear here, faith over fear!" I began to feel faith and strength entering my heart.

In Pursuit of His Presence

My Prayer with You

Dear Lord, help me to change my mindset and attitude about my future. Relieve all this anxiety and fear today. Thank you for bringing order in my life, the nation, and this world. I know that you are still in control. Amen.

Reading: Joshua 1:6-9

TRACK YOUR STEPS:

DAY 22

RESET AND SHIFT

Set your affection on things above, not on things on the earth.

Colossians 3:2

Reset and shift is a computer term that occurs when a change is needed to start a new phase. Likewise, we experience these two events on a daily basis. We experience daily transition from one situation to another. Transition from home to work, then work to home. The seasons transition from one season to another. We have to reset our thinking, to make a successful transition to a different environment. Don't forget and leave the reset button home.

There was a commercial advertising a new feature on a new computer design. This reset may be needed throughout our day, or a period in time when you are a child of God, he will reset your direction. Be open to the reset and shift that God wants to do in your life.

My Prayer with You

Dear Lord, reset me for your Glory. I am willing to follow your direction. Amen.

Reading: Ephesians 3:23, Isaiah 40:5-13

TRACK YOUR STEPS:

In Pursuit of His Presence

DAY 23

A TIME FOR REST

The Lord replied, "My Presence will go with you, and I will give you rest."

Exodus 33:14

Rest is to cease from work or movement in order to relax and refresh yourself or recover strength. To be placed or supported so as to stay in a specific position. The Hebrew word for rest is nuach- to rest, to be quiet. Sometimes it is synonymous to Shabat - to cease or to rest. Sabbath day of rest. The Greek word for Rest is refresh.

There are different types of rest, spiritual, physical, and mental. Spiritual rest in Matthew 11:29, Jesus tells us how to get rest and learn about him. He is our rest. A rest for our soul. Physical rest is the most important rest. Physical rest is Sleep. Sleep provides restorative benefits. Mental rest is when you notice that you need to defog your brain. It's when your thoughts on things don't edify. Prayer and devotions bring the peace needed.

My Prayer with You

Dear, Heavenly Father. On this day of rest. I have been feeling physically tired, and mentally depleted but now spending time in your presence I am spiritually refreshed. Amen.

In Pursuit of His Presence

Reading: Matthew 6:33

TRACK YOUR STEPS:

DAY 24

STAY FOCUSED...LEARN THE LESSON

When our enemies heard that we were aware of their plot and that God had frustrated it, we all returned to the wall, each to our own work.

Nehemiah 4:15

Nehemiah found a way to complete the task before him. He stayed committed to his God given assignment. He was focused. Focus is to gather all of your attention, concentration, and to be centered around one objective. A lot has been said and written about multitasking, but research has proven that you can achieve quality and quantity when you are single-minded.

We see in these chapters there were many distractions that came to them, but they addressed the problems then returned to the work. It was completed in 52 days. In the mist of great opposition, Nehemiah remained committed to God and those he was sent to serve.

My Prayer with You

Dear Heavenly Father, help me through the Holy Spirit to be focused, to rise above the distractions, the world, the flesh (my selfish desires), and the adversary it brings into my life. Amen.

Reading: Nehemiah 4:1- 5:1

In Pursuit of His Presence

TRACK YOUR STEPS:

DAY 25

ELIMINATION

To everything there is a season, and a time to every purpose under the heaven.

Ecclesiastes 3:1

There are moments in our journey that God wants to make some changes in our life. The change is to equip us for what is in the future. Have you ever heard of an elimination diet? It works by removing certain foods for a while to determine if it is the allergic reaction or problem. Some of those substances can cause health concerns and even lead to death if they remain. In a true elimination diet the food eliminated may be reintroduced to determine if that specific substance or food is the trigger.

In the natural as it is in the spiritual, God takes things away from us because it is not doing anything for our good, growth, and maturity. The time for that person and habit has come to an end in our life. Have you noticed the elimination of things? Don't fight against it, but ask God about it. He will show you why it is happening and what he is doing. He will replace what was removed with the right things, for that time.

In Pursuit of His Presence

My Prayer with You

Dear Heavenly Father, give me discernment when things, people, places, or plans change. Help me to understand my season. I want to please you and be in your Perfect will. Amen.

Reading: Ecclesiastes 3:1-11

TRACK YOUR STEPS:

DAY 26

FELLOWSHIP AND UNITY

For God has not given us a spirit of fear, but of power and of love and of a sound mind.

2 Timothy 1:7

This song of ascent was written by King David, when the children of Israel traveled to the city of Jerusalem, they sang a number of songs. On their way to worship in the temple, they were required to maintain the three high holy days or festivals each year.

One Saturday, we gathered in the fellowship hall of our Church to serve the saints who were unable to come out because of the COVID-19, coronavirus. There is a saying that "many hands make light work."

That means when we work together, on a large task, it can be done quickly and efficiently. There we were in the fellowship hall with more than enough to serve. We talked and laughed. When the body of Christ gather together in unity God commands a blessing.

My Prayer with You

Dear Heavenly Father, I come to you in Jesus Name. Thank you for this Blessing of the family of God. Jesus prayed, that we be one. We are one in harmony and in unity. Amen.

Reading: Psalm 133:1-3

TRACK YOUR STEPS:

DAY 27

BE STILL

God is our refuge and strength, a very present help in trouble.

Psalms 46:1–11

Being still, is not only the absence of activity, but a quietness of the soul. We are triune beings with spirit, soul and body. Each one of us know what will cause our spirit to be still. Once the spirit is calm then the soul will respond, and the body will align itself.

Today, take a few minutes and set aside time to think about situations, where you saw God's hand working things out for you.

My Prayer with You

Dear, Heavenly Father, my spirit seeks after your stillness. I now yield to the Holy Spirit's peace. Thank you for stillness and peace today. Amen.

Reading: Philippians 4:8

TRACK YOUR STEPS:

In Pursuit of His Presence

DAY 28

SLOW DOWN AND SMELL THE ROSES

For we are to God the pleasing aroma of Christ among those who are being saved and those who are perishing.

2 Corinthians 2:15

Slow Down and Smell the Roses are words from a song. It is a song from many years ago and it still holds true today. The years before COVID-19, were so fast pace and hectic that I didn't know if I was coming or going. I just could not keep up. I was always on the go until I felt a nudge in my heart to shut things down and be alone with God.

I needed to hear his voice, to gather my thoughts and to gain strength. We are a fragrance of Christ in God's nostril. When we take time to consecrate our life to God, grow in his grace, and to stand strong in faith. We exude an aroma.

That fragrance permeates the atmosphere. All of the stench of the world, the flesh, and the enemy of our soul dissipates when God is near and the Holy Spirit is acknowledged. As, I sit here today, thinking the more time we spend in his presence, abiding there in the Holy Spirit, we are transformed through the power of the Holy Spirit into the image of Christ.

In Pursuit of His Presence

My Prayer with You

Dear Lord, make me a fragrance of Jesus Christ to all, I come in contact with. Amen.

Reading: 2 Corinthians 2:14-16

TRACK YOUR STEPS:

DAY 29

PURE JOY

But the fruit of the spirit is love, joy, peace, long-suffering, gentleness, goodness, faith.

Galatians 5:22

Doing things can produce happiness but Joy comes from trusting God to fill and fulfil you. Cultivate, the fruit of Joy. Bearing Joy is very necessary, and it is essential in the believer's life. Chara is the Greek word meaning Joy.

The fruit of Joy is an attribute, of the Holy Spirit bearing fruit may not come easy, but it is what I need more of. Romans 14:17 states, "weeping may tarry for the night, but joy comes in the morning." Joy can only be found in a personal living relationship with Jesus Christ. As our soul clings to Jesus Christ, we can experience his Joy. Every believer can experience His joy.

These are the benefits of Joy. Joy lifts up your spirit. It brings gratitude, it brings thanksgiving, it adjusts your attitude, and puts you in a happy place. The joy of the Lord is my strength.

My Prayer with You

Dear Lord, fill me with your Holy Spirit, I need your Joy to strengthen me daily for the journey before me. Amen.

Reading: Nehemiah 8:10

TRACK YOUR STEPS:

In Pursuit of His Presence

DAY 30

CLEAR THE RUNWAY

And shall say, Cast ye up, cast ye up, prepare the way, take up the stumbling block out of the way of my people.

Isaiah 57:14

Have you ever traveled on an airplane and looked out the window before departure, you would see the ground crew clearing the runway? Each Aircraft need a clear path to follow, so that it can depart to its designation.

Another runway is not as dramatic, but nonetheless it is a runway. The fashion shows have runways. There is fashion Mecca's in New York City's Garment district; they have runways as well. They are running out of fashion houses in NYC on Fashion Avenue. The runways there make room for the new styles to come forth for the season. This is where the last and latest fall/winter or spring/summer garments are viewed; so out with the old and in with the new.

We as believers, must keep our lives clear and free of clutter; so, others can see Jesus Christ clearly in you, and understand Him to follow him. John the Baptist did this. He was able to clear the way by heralding the way for Christ. Then, when he came on the scene, John bowed out of the way.

In Pursuit of His Presence

My Prayer with You

Dear Heavenly Father, I am asking you to help me Clear a pathway out of my life, so that you can reveal Jesus. Amen.

Reading: John 1:22-23

TRACK YOUR STEPS:

DAY 31

20/20 IS HINDSIGHT

Nevertheless, the righteous will hold to their ways, and those with clean hands will grow stronger.

Job 17:9

The old adage, hindsight is 20/20, is an English idiom which means that I should have paid more attention. 20/20 is good vision and the set goal is to correct a person who wears eyeglasses to 20/20.

Looking back in the past can have some benefits. You can gain strength and insight into what happened and how to navigate the present and future. Remember to move forward. Lot's wife looked back and it caused her to turn into a pillar of salt, in essence a hard stone. Have you looked back? She lost out on a new thing God could have done in her life. Don't be like her. Move forward!

My Prayer with You

Dear Lord God, I am acknowledging that I have made many mistakes and was hurt by them. Forgive and cleanse me from all unrighteousness. I desire to move forward not looking back anymore. I give you glory, honor, and praise. Amen.

Reading: Genesis 19:26

TRACK YOUR STEPS:

ACKNOWLEDGMENTS

This devotional is a collaborative effort initiated by the Spirit of God therefore our acknowledgements start with God. We honor him with the work of our hands and this labor of love. He has provided the talent, motivation, and discipline to finish this project. We also acknowledge our families for their love and patience as we threw ourselves into this collection of insights and reflections. To our ministry families- we need and appreciate cheerleaders. Thank you for the support and encouragement as we strive to globally impact the Kingdom of God. We also take this opportunity to acknowledge and thank the bishops and staff of the Southern Assembly Churches of Christ Disciples of Christ Eastern District of America, our individual pastors and mentors for their guidance, and for all that they have poured into us. To our publisher, Push-A-Pencil Publishing, we say bravo to the spirit of excellence. What great things the Lord has in store for you. Finally, we acknowledge and recognize Dr. Constance Hamilton-McCloud who was inspired by the Holy Spirit and birthed the idea. We are indeed In Pursuit of His Presence. We pray that the God inspired words of this devotional are a blessing to each of you.

About the Authors

Trudy Askew-Robinson is a teacher by training and a shepherd by Kingdom assignment. Her burden for The Kingdom includes teaching and preaching the Word of God so that people's hearts are turn to God; that the body of Christ be fully equipped for the work of ministry and to cultivate kingdom warriors. She currently serves as pastor of St Paul Church of Christ Ayden NC. Trudy is an East Carolina University Alumna and current graduate student. She is a proud mother of two and a doting grandmother. Her favorite scripture is Psalm 27:4 "One thing have I desired of the Lord, that will I seek after; that I may dwell in the house of the Lord all the days of my life, to behold the beauty of the Lord, and to enquire in his temple."

Dr. Constance Hamilton-McCloud is an ordained Elder in the Church of Christ Disciples of Christ church. She is an associate Elder at St Paul Church of Christ in Ayden, NC. She has a master's degree in Theology and Ministry. She also holds a bachelor's degree in Theology and graduated from Covenant Theological Seminary. Her calling is to teach and proclaim the Word of God in its totality.

Tonya Parker-Davis is the Senior Pastor of New Life Church of Christ in Greenville NC, and she is the founder of Tonya P. Davis Ministries. Her objective in life is to fulfill her God given destiny, and to motivate others to do the same. Tonya holds a Master of Theology degree and a Master of Science degree with a concentration in Nursing; she is also a certified case manager. She is currently in pursuit of a doctorate degree in Christian Church leadership. She is happily married to the love of her life, Deacon Gary Lenn Davis, Sr. They have two children. Her favorite scripture is John 9:4 "I must work the works of Him that sent me while it is day: the night cometh, when no man can work."

In Pursuit of His Presence

www.ingramcontent.com/pod-product-compliance
Lightning Source LLC
Chambersburg PA
CBHW031212090426
42736CB00009B/892